DRUGS AND CRIME

In South America, drug lords like Pablo Escobar became
extremely powerful because of the large quantities of drugs he
controlled.

THE DRUG ABUSE PREVENTION LIBRARY

DRUGS AND CRIME

Victor Adint

THE ROSEN PUBLISHING GROUP, INC.
NEW YORK

Published in 1994 by The Rosen Publishing Group, Inc.
29 East 21st Street, New York, NY 10010

First Edition

Manufactured in the United States of America

Library of Congress Cataloging-in-Publication Data

Adint, Victor
    Drugs and crime / Victor Adint—1st ed.
    p.   cm.—(The Drug abuse prevention library)
    Includes bibliographical references and index.
      ISBN 0-8239-1539-5
      1. Drug abuse and crime—United States—Juve-
    nile literature. 2. Drug abuse—United States—
    Prevention—Juvenile literature. 3. Youth—
    United States—Drug use—Juvenile literature.
    [1. Drug abuse.] I. Title. II. Series.
    HV5825.A665   1994
    364.2'4—dc20   93-41862
                                      CIP
                                      AC

Contents

Introduction

*T*his book is designed to help you make the most important decision of your life— whether to get involved in drugs and crime or not. Other people can tell you not to get involved, but you have to decide. I am not going to tell you what to do. All I want to do is give you the information that you need to make your own decision. Drug dealers and gang members will tell you only half the truth. This book tells you what dealers don't want you to know.

If you are already involved in drugs and crime, this book can help you better understand the drug business. If you plan to stay in the business, this book might help you survive a little longer. Chances are you haven't been involved long enough to know what is really going on. You might even decide to get out. That would *greatly* improve your chances of survival.

CHAPTER 1

Street Drugs

Drugs are everywhere. Doctors prescribe them for patients, people buy them at the corner drugstore, and pushers sell them on the street. Drug dealers want you to believe that the drugs they sell are safe. The truth is that drug dealers don't know.

Legal prescription drugs are made in recognized laboratories. Doctors and pharmacologists spend a lot of time making sure the drugs are safe and effective. They have the equipment and the knowledge necessary to do that.

Prescription drugs may help someone recover from an illness, but those same drugs can be very dangerous for some

8 | other person. Only the patient can legally and safely take the drug prescribed. If someone else takes it, that use is unsafe and sometimes illegal.

Prescription drugs are sometimes sold on the streets. Drug dealers steal them, or people sell their own prescriptions. These drugs are usually tampered with. Even if they are not tampered with, they are still dangerous because their use is not supervised by a physician.

Chemists and Cooks

Street drugs are *always* illegal. They are not made in recognized laboratories. They are usually made in kitchens, bathrooms, or basements of homes or in abandoned buildings. The people who run the drug businesses are called "chemists." Those who make the drugs are called "cooks."

Anybody can be a cook. Cooks are trained by other cooks while making drugs. They don't need to go to college. Cooks combine dangerous chemicals to try to make marketable drugs like LSD, PCP, and amphetamines. D-lysergic acid diethylamide (LSD) is a hallucinogenic drug more commonly known as "acid." Phencyclidine (PCP) is also a hallucinogenic, known as "angel dust."

Most of the illegal drugs sold on the street are prepared in kitchens, bathrooms, or abandoned buildings.

10 Amphetamine and methamphetamine are stimulants known as "meth," "crank," "speed," and "ice." Ice is a crystal form of amphetamine that is smoked. MDMA (Ecstasy) is made from amphetamine; it also causes hallucinations.

Cooks don't know if they made the drug right until someone uses it. Some of the chemicals they use are very expensive and hard to find. If they make a batch of a drug that turns out wrong, they usually sell it anyway. Many people have died from taking a drug from a bad batch.

Other street drugs such as cocaine, heroin, and marijuana come from plants. Cocaine and heroin have to be extracted from the plant and processed. Marijuana does not need to be processed.

Cocaine

Cocaine comes from coca leaves. The leaves are mixed with kerosene, acetone, or gasoline and then soaked and mashed to extract a paste. The paste is refined into cocaine hydrochloride, and the left-over substance containing leaf pulp and kerosene or gasoline is separately sold as "basuka," which means trash. The name basuka was changed to "bazooka" when the stuff was brought to the United States.

Bazooka is smoked. It is considered to be the most dangerous form of cocaine.

Cocaine hydrochloride is a powder that is usually inhaled through the nose or injected in a vein. It is mixed and diluted with sugars and local anesthetics. Drugs are mixed or diluted with similar looking substances to increase their bulk and profit. A diluted drug is said to be "cut," "stepped on," or "hit." Crack or freebase is produced from cocaine hydrochloride and baking soda or ether. The result is a smokable solid or "rock" cocaine. Cocaine is highly addictive.

Heroin

Heroin is obtained from opium. Opium comes from a special kind of poppy seed pod. Heroin is commonly cut with powdered milk, sugars, and starch. It is highly addictive. On the street heroin is commonly called "horse," "China white," and "Mexican brown."

Marijuana

Marijuana is also referred to as "pot," "weed," "grass," and "ganja." It comes from the leaves of the cannabis plant. Tetrahydrocannabinol or THC is the chemical that creates the high. Drugs like PCP,

12 | hashish oil, and cocaine are commonly added to make the marijuana more powerful. Hashish oil also comes from the cannabis plant and can contain up to 20 percent THC.

Unlike prescription drugs, street drugs can be sold by anyone to anyone. The street dealer cannot guarantee that the drug was made properly and doesn't know if the buyer will be seriously hurt by using it. The street dealer is not directly involved in making the drug and may never meet the chemist or dealer. The quality and strength of the drug are totally unpredictable. No one knows its effect until someone takes it. A drug user puts his or her life in the hands of the dealer and all the other people who handled the drug. Taking too much of a drug can result in an overdose and possible death.

Think about it. When you visit your doctor you place your health and life in the hands of a trained professional. The doctor may prescribe a safe and predictable drug to help improve your health. Are you prepared to do the same with a street dealer who probably knows less about drugs than you do after having read this chapter?

CHAPTER 2

Drugs Are Big Business

*T*he drug business can be compared to a kingdom. There are people at the top, people in the middle, and people at the bottom. Only the "royal family" possess the real power. Those in the middle are few, and those at the bottom are many. You can't start at the bottom and make it to the top. You have to be "family" to be trusted by a drug lord. When I use the word "royal," I don't mean it in a romantic way. The only thing similar is the power. There are no knights performing good deeds in the drug kingdom. The only loyalty is personal gain and survival. People in the business are not loyal to others out of love or duty. They are only loyal out of fear.

14 | *Heroin, Cocaine, and Marijuana*

Drug lords live in other countries where they grow, harvest, and process cocaine, heroin, and marijuana in large quantities. Drugs are big business, and the money the drug lords make buys them a lot of power. They hire their own armies and pay off government officials. The United States Drug Enforcement Agency cannot arrest them unless their government cooperates or they come into the U.S.

Drug lords use local people to harvest and process the drugs. Many of these people are paid with crude forms of the drugs or with by-products (waste). Many workers who process cocaine are paid with bazooka or cocaine paste.

The drugs are shipped to the United States and received by middle-level drug smugglers. These smugglers are usually "family." Their job is to sell the drugs to distributors. The distributor cuts the drug and sells or fronts it to several dealers. Fronting is like wholesaling. When a drug is fronted to a distributor, a price is agreed upon and the distributor has to come up with the money later. If he fails to come up with the money, family or not, he is punished or killed. *There is always someone to take his place.*

Thousands of lives are lost every year because of drug-related crime.

16   The distributor then tests the drug for strength and cuts it again. "Pigs" are often used to test the drugs. Pigs are people who want to get into the business. They are told that taking the drug is part of their initiation. Many of them do not survive the initiation. The drug is then sold or fronted to dealers who control certain city or rural areas. The drug is tested again and cut. The dealers then recruit gangs or street dealers to sell the drug to the users.

Street dealers or gangs who work for dealers are fronted drugs to sell. They are required to sell the drugs and return the money to the dealer running their area. Street dealers are usually given a small amount of the drug to sell for their own profit. Street dealers end up in jail, addicted to drugs, or dead more frequently than anybody else in the drug business. The ones who become addicted are not trusted by those higher in the ranks and often end up dead. The chances for a street dealer to advance and become a low-level distributor are almost zero. Street dealers know this, and it adds to the pressure of doing their job. All they care about is selling the drugs and improving their chances of promotion.

Police in Colombia, South America, spray fields of poppies with chemicals to destroy the crop.

One person's choice to use drugs can affect many innocent people. This subway car derailed because the conductor was under the influence of drugs.

There are two ways a street dealer can **19** move up in the business. One is to live long enough for someone else to end up dead or in jail. The other is to buy in large quantities and start his own operation. A dealer who starts an operation, however, is almost immediately marked for death by other dealers and street gangs. Competition is not appreciated.

PCP, LSD, Ecstasy, and Amphetamine

Drugs like LSD, PCP, Ecstasy, and amphetamines are primarily produced in the United States. They are made in small illegal factories. The operation is much smaller than for heroin, cocaine, and marijuana. The police have a hard time finding the smaller places.

Once the drugs are made by the cooks, they are packaged and sold by the chemists to the distributors or dealers. The actual drug transaction is always done away from the factory. Chemists don't trust the people they do business with and will not give away their location. The drugs then enter the main drug distribution system.

While I worked at a county jail as a drug-abuse counselor, I once counseled a cook. The police had busted his operation,

20 and he was doing time. He wanted to get out of the business and off the drugs. I remember his telling me that cooks never really get out of the business. They know valuable trade secrets, and they know the major chemists. He was a great guy when he was clean and not working as a cook. I spent a lot of time trying to help him. He intended to move away and continue his recovery when he got out of jail. I thought he had a chance, but I was wrong. They found him. The last I heard, he was working as a cook again.

Money in the Business

People who make money in the drug business and live in the United States have a hard time spending it. All income is taxed by the government. Drug money is made by criminal activity. If a dealer pays taxes on drug income he admits to the crime of dealing drugs. If he doesn't pay taxes on the income, the government charges him with tax evasion. High-level drug dealers set up honest businesses, like retail stores, so they can claim their drug money as legal income. The drug money is then taxed along with the money from the business, and they can spend it. This is called laundering money.

It may be tempting for some teens to accept drugs from friends, but it is wiser to say no.

The U.S. Drug Enforcement Agency seizes tons of illegally imported drugs every year.

Federal law says that any property owned by a drug dealer can be seized by the government if the government can prove that it was paid for or partly paid for with drug money. Drug dealers who don't have a way to launder their money can't spend it easily. They keep large amounts of cash and hope that they will be able to find a way.

I counseled a guy one time who had an interesting way of laundering his money. He had a stockbroker who would take his drug money and give him clean money at the rate of fifty cents on the dollar. The broker gave him a statement indicating that the money was stock dividends. He could then be taxed on the money and spend it freely. His scheme worked for a while, but it was eventually discovered and he went to jail.

Other Kinds of Crime

Drug dealers are criminals and have no problem committing other crimes. In fact, it's absolutely necessary. Dealers accept stolen merchandise as payment for drugs. Most drug addicts don't have money. They have to steal it or sell some of their "stash" (supply of drug for personal use) to buy more. Drug addicts rob houses and stores

24 and trade the stolen property for drugs. A $500 stolen TV can be sold to a dealer for 10 percent (or less) of its worth. The drug user gets $50 worth of drugs. The dealer sells the stolen TV for 50 to 70 percent of its worth.

Murder is commonplace in the drug business. Carrying a gun is frequently necessary. Most of the guns used in the business are stolen property. Dealers don't buy their guns legally because legal guns are easier to trace. Dealers frequently buy, sell, and trade stolen guns.

Dealers are frequently involved in prostitution. Some addicts will sell their bodies for drugs. The drug dealer either buys sex with drugs or sells an addict to someone else. Many young people who use drugs and become addicted end up as prostitutes. Both boys and girls are used in prostitution. They are often forced to participate in perverted forms of sex. A girl who trades sex for drugs is commonly called a "strawberry." Boys and girls are said to be "turned out" if they trade sex for drugs. Boys are more often bought by older men. Girls are bought by men more often than by women. Someone who is turned out gets little or no respect in the business and is frequently abused.

As drug use has grown, street gangs have taken over much of the drug dealing that happens on city streets.

Drug dealers can't go to the police if someone rips them off. They can't rely on the police to protect them from rival dealers. They use gang members or create a gang to act as the strong arm of the business. The dealers do the same thing as the drug lords in other countries. They hire or create their own armies.

25

Drug-awareness programs have become an important part of our educational system.

CHAPTER 3

Drugs, Crime, and Youth

The drug business requires people to take risks. No risk, no money. As the risk increases, the level of trust among people in the business decreases. Drug enforcement is getting tougher, and the sentences for drug crimes are longer. Dealers and gang members are less willing to do their own dirty work.

Adolescents are treated different by the law. The criminal justice system is much easier on them. Dealers would rather let teenagers "take the fall" (be arrested). A younger person is easier to scare and control. Dealers are less concerned about being double-crossed. Younger and younger boys and girls are being recruited

27

28 into the business. Young people work as lookouts, spotters, couriers, dealers, enforcers, prostitutes, and pigs.

Lookouts do just that. They keep an eye on the street. If they see an unfamiliar face, they warn the dealer. They look for cops and rival dealers or gangs.

Spotters are usually used at the sales location. They don't sell the drug or possess it. Spotters direct drug users to an ideal place where they can buy drugs. The dealers might be on the roof of a building and use a piece of string and a can to exchange drugs for money. They may also use rooms that have access to the street. A dealer barricades any obvious entryways, keeps an open escape route, and makes a small opening in a wall or a barricaded door to pass drugs to and receive money from the users. If the police bust the operation, the dealer has a good chance of getting away. The spotter runs the highest risk of being arrested.

Couriers carry drugs around town. Who would suspect a 12-year-old boy or girl on a bicycle of carrying drugs? Most of the time the kids are not told what's in the bag and warned not to look. They're just given five or ten dollars and told to take it somewhere.

Young dealers sell drugs in small amounts to other kids. As they get older they may be trusted with larger amounts to sell.

Enforcers are generally gang members. Gangs are recruited or created to control certain areas. They keep out competition, increase the sales territory, collect debts, protect the dealer, and guard the operation from theft. Gang members are always highly visible and attract the attention of the police. They are also very expendable. They tend to last from one day to two years. Many of them end up physically hurt, in jail, addicted to drugs, or dead.

Young prostitutes are called "slaves" because they are owned by people in the business. They don't have a choice and can't say no. People who buy sex don't want to get AIDS. AIDS can be transmitted through sex and by sharing needles. Men and women who have been "pulling tricks" (prostituting) for a long time and who do drugs are more likely to have AIDS. Dealers believe that a young boy or girl is safer because he or she has had little or no sexual experience. Because of the danger of AIDS, more and more young boys and girls are being recruited into prostitution or slavery.

Everyone can get together to rally against drugs and crime in their neighborhood.

Teenagers at a Disadvantage

Most teenagers and parents survive growing up; most parents try to understand
their children and accept them as unique
individuals. They allow them more responsibility, and give them the love and
support they need. However, many young
people are unhappy with their lives.
Growing up is not always easy, and some
have it worse than others. Feeling misun-
derstood and wanting to rebel is a normal
part of being young. To grow up, teenagers have to slowly move away from their
parents and the control of other authority
figures. They need to learn how to make
their own decisions. When parents are un-
willing to let their kids grow up, teenagers
sometimes make poor decisions. These
decisions are based on anger and rebellion. All teenagers are in danger of
recruitment for drug activity when they
are rebelling. Those from poorer homes
have a harder time and find drugs and
crime more attractive.

Young people who live in families
where they are abused (physically or sexually) or neglected have it the hardest. They
don't have a healthy support system to
help them reach their goals in acceptable
ways. Many young people who live in

Drug-free zones discourage dealers and gangs from selling drugs near schools.

inner-city areas or ghettos feel trapped. The idea of completing school and getting a good job may seem impossible. They may see the drug business as the only way out. Some of them decide that drugs may help them cope with their lives or that a gang may take the place of their family.

Recruitment

Drug dealers and gang members have no trouble finding recruits. Some young people jump at the chance to be involved. Others are tricked or forced into the business. Disadvantaged youths are the most vulnerable to recruiters.

Drugs can be very attractive. Just using them is rebellious. Teens may find that drugs give them temporary self-esteem and relief from emotional pain. Drugs seem to help at first, but they quickly turn against the users. Users become dependent on the drug and eventually addicted.

Soon drugs stop working as well as they used to, and the addicts need more to get relief. Then, when they can't afford the drugs, they will do just about anything to get them. Many addicts steal property, deal drugs, and sell their bodies to support their habit. They are looked down on by other people in the business.

Attraction

34 Drug dealers recruit by attraction. People who see drugs as the only way to make money are easily drawn into the business. They start by getting to know a dealer and then do jobs like being a lookout, a spotter, a courier, and possibly a pig. If they survive this and do their jobs well, they are eventually trusted to deal drugs in small quantities. Young people who get involved in this way are in it for their own gain so they are more likely to cross the dealer. Dealers know this and try to keep them from being too successful. So long as the teenager needs the dealer, the dealer can control and use him or her.

Trickery

Drug dealers recruit by trickery. They befriend a teenage boy, for example, who seems vulnerable. They spend time with him, and give him money. The dealer wants the youth to turn against his parents and rely on him for emotional and physical needs. The dealer becomes a second parent and at first may do a better job than the real parents.

When the teenager feels obligated, the dealer asks him to do favors. Before too long, the teenager is carrying drugs, being a lookout, a spotter, or a pig, and dealing drugs to his friends. Dealers like to recruit this way because the youth does the favors out of gratitude and friendship. He is not out for personal gain, so he is less likely to cross the dealer. As the youth begins to realize that he is being used, the dealer regains control by getting him hooked on drugs and introducing him to prostitution.

Gang Recruiting

Gang leaders also recruit by attraction. Some teenagers have given up on school and getting a good job. They lack purpose and a feeling of importance. They may feel lost. Teenagers who lack a loving and understanding family feel a great deal of emptiness. Everybody needs something to work for and needs to feel important.

In the beginning, a gang can give a teenager a sense of purpose, importance, hope, and family unity. Later, the youth finds that the unity, loyalty, and love quickly dissolve. You don't make your own decisions in a gang. You're either in or out. You do what they want you to do, or you are rejected and punished. The gang's unity, loyalty, and love depend on your *obedience*; there is no freedom. Gang members are forced to do things that go

36 against their beliefs. A gang member has to turn his back on himself.

People who want to be in gangs generally hang out with gang members. They get in by doing favors. When they prove that they are loyal or deserve respect, they are accepted. To do that, they have to do something that hurts them or puts them in danger. They have to show that the gang is more important than they are. This is called "initiation." The gang won't trust them unless they are willing to put the gang's needs ahead of their own.

The Trap

The drug business becomes a trap for many people who are drawn in by the idea of money, power, freedom, and happiness. Once they're in, many people realize that the business is not what they expected.

Money can be made by dealing drugs. The only problem is that it's a different kind of money. Sure, it can buy nice things, but at what cost? To make money and survive, dealers and gang members have to be meaner and crueler than the next guy. A good dealer has to be able to put business before everything else.

When most young people start out in the business, they have a conscience, a

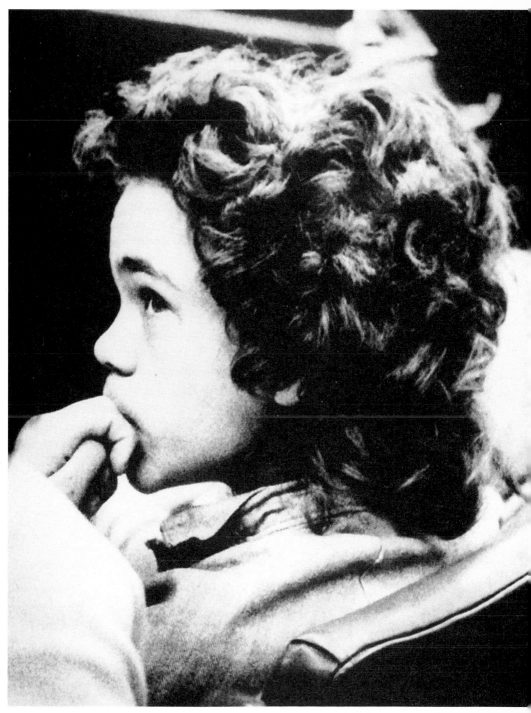

This 13-year-old boy was arrested on suspicion of dealing drugs.
The money that can be made dealing is attractive even to the very
young, but selling drugs can carry a heavy price if you're caught.

38 | sense of right and wrong. Most of them believe that they will be different. They say, "If I don't do it, someone else will. Heck, I could make a lot of money and go legit. I won't do the things other dealers or gang members do. I won't cross my friends, sell drugs to younger kids, steal from my family or friends, hurt other people, or abuse drugs and become addicted. I won't take any foolish risks, and I won't get caught by the police." What most young people don't realize is that they have to do *all* those things and *more* to survive and make it in the business.

Young people are of great importance in the drug business. The law treats them differently, and the dealers take advantage of that. Most experienced dealers have a criminal record and face longer prison terms than youths under 16 or 18.

Getting Hooked on Money

In the beginning, the youth is asked to do light work. The work has little risk (compared to other tasks) and does not require him to go seriously against his values. If the youth performs well, he is paid. The money and acceptance are rewarding at first. But the teen quickly learns that the other people are making a lot more money.

This triggers an ambition to move up in the business. As the teen becomes more attracted to the money and power, he becomes more willing to do the things he swore he would never do.

The teen is then required to do dirtier work: collections, theft, violence, vandalism, and prostitution. The teen at first may be somewhat uncomfortable with these new tasks, but he is already trapped. By now the youth is addicted to the business and totally hooked on the money. He is afraid to disappoint the dealer or gang, and terrified of being rejected or thought of as not "cool." To continue in the business, the teen has to change all of his values and shut off his emotions. Feelings get in the way. They make him feel bad about what he's doing and less able to do what it takes to succeed and survive in the business. The youth must *isolate* himself from his feelings and ignore or change his values and morals.

Losing Trust and Friendship

As he moves up in the business, the teen learns that he can't trust anyone. Everyone wants to make more money and have more power. Teens are loyal to one another only if they can benefit from that

40 loyalty. If they believe that crossing some-one will bring them more benefit than harm, they'll do it. A successful dealer has to make others fear him and believe that they will benefit from working for him.

Friendships cease to matter. The youth learns to isolate himself from others because he can't trust their friendship. He can't trust anyone with his feelings and thoughts because they might be used against him. If he allows himself to care about people in the business, he will be hurt if they cross him or feel the pain of loss if they are killed. He may even have to kill his own friend out of duty to his dealer or gang, or to gain more fear and respect from his peers. Loved ones who are not in the business are also a threat. If a boss wants to punish him or make him do something he doesn't want to do, the boss goes after his friends and family.

If you think about it, the youth is already in jail. He has turned his back on his own values, morals, and feelings. He is isolated because he can't allow himself close friendships. No matter how much money he has, it's not enough. He constantly has to make sure he isn't being crossed. He also has to worry about being caught by the police. If he spends his

Drug dependency will eventually ruin your life.

money carelessly, the government will bust him for tax evasion or seize his property.

A dealer who wants to get out of the business finds it almost impossible. People in the business don't like it when someone tries to go straight. They worry that he may talk to the police. If a dealer is making a profit for others, they might not allow the person to get out until he is no longer useful to them. *The money made in the business carries an enormous price.*

Depending on the judge, young people can either serve time in a juvenile facility or be placed in an institution with adult criminals.

CHAPTER 4

Busted

What hapens when you get busted? Every juvenile court has broad authority when deciding on suitable punishment for adolescents. Judges have flexibility when making a decision on a particular case. Juvenile courts generally give adolescents more opportunities for rehabilitation than adult courts.

Getting busted as a juvenile is not a "cakewalk." Juveniles get less protection from the law. It's easier for a juvenile to be convicted of a crime. Jail or incarceration terms are based on the same penal codes used for adults.

Juvenile criminal files are not automatically sealed when an adolescent turns 18.

44 An adolescent has to ask the court to have his file sealed. If an adolescent continues to get in trouble with the law after the age of 18, his file remains open.

Different Courts

There are many differences between juvenile and adult courts. Unsupported testimony of an accomplice can be used against a minor. That means a police officer may not have to find someone to back up an accomplice's story. The story may be used against the adolescent in court. A juvenile can be arrested on a misdemeanor charge without a warrant, even if the officer didn't see the adolescent commit the crime and wasn't in the immediate area. If an adolescent commits a crime and gets away, an officer can arrest the adolescent if there is good reason to believe he committed the crime. To arrest an adult in the same situation, a police officer has to get permission from a judge (a warrant). Adolescents do not have a right to bail. If an adolescent is locked up, he is not permitted to pay bail to get out while waiting for a jurisdictional hearing or disposition. A jurisdictional hearing is the same thing as a trial in an adult court. Most juvenile courts use the word "disposition" instead of "sentence." The judge decides whether the adolescent must be locked up until a jurisdictional hearing or disposition. Only four states allow jury trials for adolescents.

The Same Laws

Adolescents are prosecuted under the same laws as adults and jail time is based on the same penal codes used for adults. The only differences are that most adolescents are not given the maximum penalty for their crime and usually do their time in a juvenile facility. Juvenile facilities, also called juvenile hall, are county jails for adolescents. State youth authorities are penitentiaries for adolescents.

Juveniles can be tried as adults. Youths under the age of 16 are assumed to be fit for trial in juvenile court. If the district attorney wants the case to be handled by the adult court, he or she has to prove that the youth is unfit to be tried in juvenile court. If the youth is over 16, his defense attorney must prove that the case is fit to be handled by the juvenile court.

In either case, the juvenile court judge makes the decision. This decision is based on the severity of the crime, previous crimes committed, and previous arrests.

Adolescent offenders are punished by the court under the same laws used for adults.

The laws in most states are being changed |
to make it easier for adolescents to be
tried in adult courts. More adolescents are
committing serious crimes, and more of
them are being tried in adult courts.

Most crimes that lead to an adolescent's
being tried in an adult court are crimes of
violence. Those are crimes in which someone is killed, seriously injured, raped, or
kidnapped, and in which a gun or other
dangerous weapon is used. If the youth is
caught selling, trafficking, preparing, or
making a large amount of a drug, he or
she can be tried in an adult court. Each
case is looked at separately. If the teen is
convicted in an adult court, he or she can
be sentenced to an adult facility or to a
juvenile facility.

Juvenile Penalties

Most adolescents are given several chances
to get their act together, unless they have
committed a serious crime. There are
many programs to help young people get
back on track. Charges can be dismissed
if a youth gets counseling and does not
commit another offense. For a first or second minor offense, the sentence may be a
short stay in a juvenile detention facility
and probation requiring counseling and

48 good behavior. Probation often requires random testing and drug-abuse counseling if drugs were involved in the crime. If the youth offends again or commits a serious crime, his time in juvenile hall increases and the probation rules become more strict. Most counties have work farms as a last step before sending a youth to a state youth authority.

In juvenile court, the word "petition" is used instead of "criminal charges." Drug selling is a felony. You don't have to be in possession of a large amount of drugs to be charged and convicted of drug sales. A teen can be charged with drug sales if he has a pager or a "pay/owe sheet" and a large amount of cash. A pay/owe sheet is a piece of paper or book with names and numbers of people owed or paid money. Young people who are found guilty of or admit to drug sales or trafficking petition receive much heavier penalties.

Many adolescents take advantage of the second chance they are given and do get back on track. Others laugh at the penalties and don't realize that things quickly get much worse. At first the penalties are less than those in an adult court because the court wants to help young people. Most judges realize that youths who com-

mit crimes are often abused, neglected, or
troubled and need help, not just punishment. If the teen continues to commit
crimes, however, he can be treated like an
adult criminal. He will receive a longer
sentence and be sent to a state youth authority or in some cases, an adult jail or
penitentiary.

Choosing to live without drugs means a happier and healthier life for you and those around you.

What Now?

Many young people get into the drug business without knowing what it's all about. They mistakenly believe that it's a way to improve their lives. Having read this book, you have the information. Now it's your job to make a decision. No one else can make it for you.

Gang members, dealers, and drug users will tell you that what you have read is not true. Either they don't want to admit what's really going on, or they haven't been involved long enough to know. People who commit crimes try to justify it by convincing themselves that it is okay. By lying to themselves, they hold on to the belief that the drug business can create miracles.

52 This is called *denial*. When dealers and gang members realize that the drug business is not a way to improve their life, they are trapped and find it difficult to get out.

I am not going to tell you what to do. When adults try to make decisions for you, they rob you of your power. I'm going to let you in on a secret. You are not just a powerless teenager in a confusing adult world. You are not owned by your parents or by society. Your parents and society are supposed to be there to support and encourage you as you grow up. Adults are needed to help you make important decisions until you learn how to make good decisions for yourself.

As young people grow up, they want to become more independent. If they are not allowed to make decisions on their own, they feel a need to rebel. This is completely normal. The problem is that some young people destructively instead of constructively rebel in trying to claim their rights.

Giving Away Your Power

Young people who rebel *destructively* against their school, their parents, and society give their power away. Think about it. When we do what others don't want us to do just to upset them, we allow them to determine our behavior. Instead of choosing for ourselves, we end up choosing what the authority figures don't want us to do. Young people who do that are hurting themselves more than anyone else. They are the ones who end up with a drug problem, no education, in jail.

Drug dealers and gang members will try to decide for you. They will support your rebellion and lie to you about the business. They will try to influence you by peer pressure and fear. If you become addicted, the drug will take over your life. An addict's decisions are made by the need for drugs. If you get involved in the business, you will eventually find that your *life* decisions are made for you.

Make Your Own Decisions

Take back your power. This is *constructive* rebellion! If you make the decision to do well in school and stay out of the business, do it for yourself. If you do it for yourself, you will feel important and you will be successful and happy in life. If you do it for someone else, you will be trapped by their expectations of you.

If you are abused by your parents, you can still take back your power. If you have

54 a parent who abuses you physically, sexually, or emotionally, you have the right to defend yourself. You are a human being, and you don't deserve to have *anyone* abuse you. The government is obligated to protect you. Go to the police, your school counselor, or other relatives and adults and tell them what's happening. If you continue to talk about what is happening at home, the authorities will be able to help you. Things might get worse before they get better. You might be abused more and told not to talk. But don't stop! Tell the counselor, teacher, or police officer that this is happening. A good counselor, teacher, or police officer will try to protect you. If the adult you talked to doesn't help, talk to someone else. The worst thing you can do is accept what's happening and not demand your right to help and protection. There are programs that are designed to help abused children and to help parents stop abusing their children. If you are committed to doing something with your life, no one can stop you unless you let them.

If you feel put down by society, take back your power. Take responsibility for your education. If you don't think that you're getting a good education, do some-

thing about it. Talk to your teachers and
school counselors. You will probably find
teachers who will be excited by your desire
to learn. Many young people get a poor
education because they think they're going
to school to please adults. They do only
what they need to do to get by. If you
want a good education, demand one.
There's a good chance you'll get it. If you
have a good education you will have a better chance to succeed in life. You may
gain happiness, self-esteem, pride, respect,
financial freedom, and a good life.

If you're thinking about getting involved
in the drug business, keep your eyes open
and don't be hypnotized by the lies. You
know the risks you must take. You know
the danger and the pain that will follow. If
you still decide to do it to be cool and gain
acceptance, you're giving your power
away. Making decisions to gain acceptance is not freedom. And making the
wrong decisions can end your life.

Fact Sheet

State laws vary. Here is an example from **California:** The following penalties are for simple possession of the drugs specified. The penalties are much greater for possession with intent to sell, for unlawful transportation, and for inducing a minor to possess, sell, or transport the drug.

- Cocaine, heroin, 16 months, 2 years, or 3 years in state prison.
- LSD, PCP, 16 months, 2 years, or 3 years in state prison. If probation is granted, then up to 1 year in county jail.
- Marijuana (less than 1 ounce), $100 fine; (more than 1 ounce), maximum of 16 months in state prison or 6 months in county jail and $500 fine.

All of these penalties are increased under certain circumstances. If the offense involves cocaine or heroin and occurs at a church, youth center, or playground, the sentence may be enhanced by 1 year. If the offense involves cocaine or heroin and occurs on school grounds, the sentence may be enhanced by 2 years.

If the offense involves a minor who is
more than four years younger than the de-
fendant, the sentence may be enhanced by
1, 2, or 3 years at the discretion of the
court.

Selected Juvenile Crime Statistics

According to the FBI (Federal Bureau of
Investigation), 5 percent of all persons arrested in the United States in 1990 were
under the age of 15; 16 percent were under
the age of 18. Following are some of the
offenses charged and the number in each
age category.

Offense Charged	Under 15	Under 18
Drug abuse violations	8,758	64,740
Liquor law violations	10,449	122,047
Drunkenness	2,315	19,344
Robbery	8,874	32,967
Aggravated assault	14,860	51,167
Murder	283	2,555
Burglary	44,466	112,437
Stolen property (buying, receiving, possessing)	9,260	34,087
Weapons (carrying, possessing)	8,328	31,991
Prostitution	140	1,281
Runaway	60,549	138,155

Glossary
Explaining New Words

accomplice Person who helps another
to commit a crime.

admission Plea of guilty to a crime.

chemist Person who runs an illegal
drug-making operation.

cook Person who makes illegal drugs.

cross To turn someone in to the police, or
to rip someone off.

disposition The sentence or penalty in
juvenile court.

felony Serious crime, usually punished by
a prison term of more than one year.

front To give drugs to someone who will
sell them and pay for them later.

hallucinogen A drug that makes one see
and hear things that do not exist.

incarceration Putting a person in prison
or other confinement.

jurisdictional hearing Trial in juvenile
court.

money laundering Process that disguises
illegal money as legal money. It is done
by mixing drug money in the profits of
a legal business and paying taxes on it.

penitentiary State or federal prison for
serious offenders.

petition An indictment or complaint;
charges.

pig Person who uses an untested drug.
The dealer determines the strength of
the drug by seeing how it affects the
pig.

pulling tricks Selling sex for money or
drugs.

recruitment Persuading someone to join
a group or organization.

rehabilitation Restoring a person to good
health or good behavior.

step on To mix with similar-looking
subtances to increase the amount and
the profit.

strawberry Girl who trades sex for
drugs.

turned out Boy or girl who is addicted
to drugs and trades sex for drugs.

Help List

Alcoholics Anonymous World Services, Inc.
P.O. Box 459
Grand Central Station
New York, NY 10163

Children's Defense Fund
Legal Division
1520 New Hampshire Ave., NW
Washington, D.C. 20036
(202) 483-1470

Drug and Alcohol Hotline
1-800-252-6465

NAACP Legal Defense Fund
10 Columbus Circle
New York, NY 10019
(212) 586-8397

Narcotics Anonymous World Service Office
16155 Wyandotte Street
Van Nuys, CA 91406

National Institute on Drug Abuse
Information and Referral Line

1-800-662-HELP

National Juvenile Law Center

3701 Lindell Boulevard
P.O. Box 14200
St. Louis MO 63178
(314) 652-5555

PLACES TO CONTACT FOR INFORMATION

- Police department (local, county, and state offices)
- Court system (local, county, and state offices)
- Lawyers
- Law libraries

For Further Reading

Atkinson, Linda. *Your Legal Rights*. New York: Franklin Watts, 1982.

Berry, Joy. *Every Kid's Guide to the Juvenile Justice System*. Chicago: Children's Press, 1987.

Edwards, Gabrielle. *Drugs on Your Streets*. New York: Rosen Publishing Group, 1993.

McFarland, Rhoda. *Coping with Substance Abuse*. New York: Rosen Publishing Group, 1990.

Olnez, Ross, and Olnez, Patricia. *Up Against the Law: Your Rights as a Minor*. New York: Lodestar Books, 1986.

Seixas, Judith S. *Drugs: What They Are and What They Do*. New York: William Morrow and Co., 1991.

Index

About the Author

Victor Adint has worked as drug-abuse counselor and educator since 1986. He began working in outpatient and inpatient drug treatment and psychiatric facilities with adolescents, adults, and families. He went to work in an adult jail, where he developed and administrated one of the first comprehensive drug treatment programs for county jail facilities in the nation. He is now a drug and crime prevention consultant in Sacramento, California.

Photo Credits

Cover photo: © Taylor-Fabricius/Gamma-Liaison.
Photos on pages 2, 15, 37, 41, 42: AP Wide World Photos; page 9: Naquen Producciones/Gamma-Liaison; page 17: Carlos Angel/Gamma-Liaison; page 18: N. Utsumi/Gamma-Liaison; pages 21, 50: Stuart Rabinowitz; page 22: © Susan Greenwood/Gamma-Liaison; page 25: Riha/Gamma-Liaison; page 26: © John Berry/Gamma-Liaison; page 30: © Doug Burrows/Gamma-Liaison; page 32: © Ken Ross/Gamma-Liaison; page 46: © Stephen Ferry/Gamma-Liaison.

Design & Production: Blackbirch Graphics, Inc.

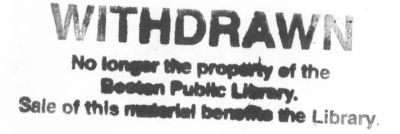